Etym(bi)ology

LIZ WALDNER

OMNIDAWN

RICHMOND, CALIFORNIA

2002

for SweetBee

*This work comes from a time, 1990-1992, when
my usual curiosity about the construction of the concept
of selfhood in american culture, and the global effects of
u.s. corporate-dominated media, coincided with an interest
in making something of it, especially with respect to my
abiding interest in the representation of women.*

Acknowledgements

Character; Black Agitator: Generator
Etym(bi)ology; Taking The "Riot" Personally: First Intensity
Rescue Work: Kenning
Still Life II: Avec
Desinit In Piscim/*A Fish Tale:* Writers From The New Coast
Descartes Ruins The World: Abacus and Five Fingers Review
Request For A Little Water Music....: 13th Moon
Melizalphabet: Abacus
Angr: Yefief
(New, Improved) Strange Matter: Crayon
A Poetics: Outlet

Book cover and interior design by Philip Krayna Design, Berkeley, California
www.pkdesign.net

Cover illustration by Jim Tucker and Liz Waldner

Library of Congress Cataloging-in-Publication Data

Waldner, Liz.
Etym(bi)ology : poems/ Liz Waldner.
   p. cm.
ISBN 1-890650-10-2 (pbk. : alk. paper)
1. Experimental poetry, American. I. Title.
PS3573.A42158 E89 2002
811'.54—dc21
            2001007567

Published by Omnidawn Publishing
Richmond, California · www.omnidawn.com · (800) 792-4957

ISBN: 1-890650-10-2 (paper)
9 8 7 6 5 4 3 2 1

Table of Contents

i.

A woman and a glass are ever in danger.
—Proverb

Even a lean pig has it in him (sic) to rage around.
—I Ching

Etym(bi)ology

"Some of them are old, some of them are new,
some of them will turn up when you least expect them to
and when they do—remember me, remember me."
—Eno

Chipped brandy snifter, crystal chrysalis, what I inherit from Athena Trasha. *Oviter dictum*: "He could only mutter, 'Darling, darling,' as he kissed the ring with the ovarian passion of the sexually dispossessed." No, not Ronald Firbank. (I am Athena Trasha you are Athena Trasha he is Athena Trasha, etc.) How do you think *gu leor* went from "enough" in Gaelic to "plentygalore" in English? A clue from Mr. Durrell: "Old Tiresias, No one half so breezy as..." "A ship without sails is like a woman without breasts."

Ok, ok, I ask you. Is it not like the streets? If more women went out at night, it would be safer for women to go out at night. (If no men went out at night, it would be safer for women to go out at night. Argument ad hominem ad hominem.) So, if more flat-chested women refrained from affixing silicone bosoms, more flat-chested women <u>could</u> refrain from affixing silicone bosoms. (If no one were deciding the value of your being based on the size of your breasts, it would be safer for women to go out at night.)

Darling, darling.
(Sexually dispossessed.)

(10)

Angr

Running around with the same two little goddam ideas IS IT
THAT THEY JUST THINK THAT OR IS IT WHAT THEY'RE
REALLY DOING? This of tonight's discussion: can people have
sex and not feel attached?

What you think, yes, it is. And isn't. De Beauvoir, *par exemple*,
smashing the dialectical diabolical clock of the equinoctial
existential—by being *une femme qui ecrit*, if you ask me

not that I ever read her
and (then o yes there's) all that *ecriture feminine* crap

I'm sorry but I've had enough where enough is too much and
Being, une femme qui ecrit, I get to say if it's true and I want to or
lie, both causes being sufficient or either or neither, I don't give a
good goddam

selah

The Catholic paper's photojournalist's mother may already at this
hour 11:17 p.m. I guess March 21 1990 be disconnected from the life
support machine an aneurism in the brain landed her in like a fish

a filament fizzled

as it did in the neck of my father who also lay
in a coma all those days—

I guess that's enough.

Although without mentioning the word vagina and my mother's record cold-shoulder how else will I explain the icicles which broke my teeth (impeded speech)?

But this is all wrong now, I no longer want to have said it April 5 I guess 1990 4:56 p.m., so now what, I have said it, and to you. I don't want to have said *vagina* either, like casuistry, a word suggestive of refrigerators and latinate fluids, edged, clinical, an ugly classical lie about me when I want to say true. My own mother. Tongue.

So now another day, November 14 1993 9:39 p.m., I could erase it all away. (Sorry Mr. Joyce's <u>Dead</u> snow goes computeresque: delete).

But I won't for the anger
as it did in the brain of my father
The same two little goddam ideas, hi I'm egg, hi I'm sperm
     write me

Rescue Work

i.

(Triage)

More people alive today than have so far died in the history of the world. Alive as verb like arrive.

Lantern   *Presage*   *Embrasure*

Who would think dumping tons of chemical weapons into the Baltic is a good way to clean up after a war? Who never had to clean up after themselves, that's who they said in the laundromat.

Mutter   *Omphalos*   *Lustrum*

Above the candelabra of new pine bough, a gas of gnats like flame, like the exhaust from living, *now* a living smoke above my head.

Armature   *Diorama*   *Steed*

ERROR IN CMOS   BAD BATTERY   BAD
CHECK SUM BAD TIME
FUNCTION

*

*

ii.

9clitoral slubtext0

Will you admit love, IS there a cross for everyone, is it *the wrestle of naming*? Bless you, watches, transits, elipses...

[chelated catechlismic]

*

...so I sd Oh Gosh and she sd Which of em do you want? in a horrid voice like glue.

[dialogic]

*

Some of yr ?'s gave some of my own a [...] —spin? spur? The uses of suggestively unintelligible handwriting. Is that it? Is suggestion innately erotic? Poetics as Erotics: The Possible...

[confessional interrogative]

*

The writing part of my brain must love her. *Placet*. Kneel down.

[professional prerogative]

*

"The 7,000 crewmen formed human letters expressing their feelings."

[inadvertent subjunctive]

*

It's not something I want to set up a tent about.
feel to L, the
void for discussion, becomes a
hat off in the house, take her
tongue of the day, on the
Philo Hall, an address

[neo-optative]

*

"Women know how to hang out with flowers,"
that kind of sitting time,
sweet space.

[delclairative lune]

*

But the enthusiasm manufacture, the Megatherium Trust, the sexual parts of flowers, beck of beck and call, plus sage que les sages: how to choose a home, how to choose a partner, *fines herbes*

3: library
4: Z
5: yoga

*

[syncretic simple(s)]

*

*

iii.

(see *sich*)

Ambulent ne tenebrae comprehendant
(a few people whose elevators are not
going all the way to the top), solo, silo, one
is one and all alone, another house,
another lark and merry frolic. From sleep
like that one awakes in shining error. I err,
I ear, I are, I or(e). (see fork)

The fork of the tree, the fork of you
(I never went in her Dodge Dart). Whole
potatoes. Concert. Barney. This/next.
Circle/line. 400 gods of drunkenness.
Canyonview. Antihistimine. Light bulb.
The house of pain. Tea. Insurance.
Requiem. At the tone. (see om)

Salvation army of the gods. Whole
populations they got so sad they poisoned
themselves. Then there were little walnut-
sized pellets for awhile. Slouching toward
Tikal. Call to pre-register. Rx. 534-1331.
Vicki? House of bone. (see home)

Pigeon   audience   caterpillars,
housewives portrait in white, strange
visitor from another planet wash basin my
eyes opened for the other to look and not
give back my hand wide sea sad voice   fish
glad to be themselves though   8:45 – 9:45
danse ordinaire make a woman of (...) yet
bleeding/sacred/our lady of eat dirt wake
up/go down/go fish/a sleep/up sleeves/creek
(see green)

"All things have rest and ripen toward the grave in silence,
    ripen fall and cease..."
    Say Sarkis say *sarx* say
    Please please please

Still Life II

*

"Rouse ye, my people...impeach the dread boss monkey and reconstruct the Happy Family." (Mark Twain)

"Ordination has been generally bad for the health of females." (Donna Haraway)

*

Benjamin and the Foucaultian Problematic, hey. Goldilocks and the Three Bears. (move from who's responsible to who's on first hey wait a minute to what are the conditions of possibility stop. interrupting me) "Someone's been sleeping in MY bed!" (small voice, and piping) (ensues the (ironic?) silence of the homeless who. like power, are thought to be everywhere and nowhere)

Power works best when it comes from below. (so much for yr Ubermensch, eh?) (MISSIONARY POSITION PROVED SUBVERSIVE—headline) Power over bodies as power to invest life with meaning. This leads to mangagement. Portfolios. And managers. Investment strategies for the dual career primatologist, I mean imperialist. Visions of the origins and the orient. Tokyo stock exchange. Babytec +22. Babylon. Merge. Reveal codes.

THE HISTORY OF DEATH Act 1, scene 2

Death as absence (where it used to mean exit, stage right, no more to strut its little while in this vale of tears) absence as presence (so

Andromache mourns Hector, *le cygne* its *beau lac natal* and Baudelaire his remembrance of Paris(s) past(s)) presence as an economically useful sexuality (everything blamed on Helen, though surely conditioning the conditions of possibility was Herr Zeus' cadeusis, the lightning rod and measure of all things incandescent prepubescent and phallocentric hegemonic universali oh shut up)

And sexuality? well, I quote: "...perfect Post Modern Man. Slithering..." [......................number of lines lost unknown] EXOTIFICATION OF THE MIDWEST (headline) STEREOTYPES POLICE MEANINGS (headline) "Erasure prelude to inscription," he sez, offstage. What has this to do with nylons? Judy Nylon? The man what couldn't afford to orgy? (sotto voce: erotization or erasure) (sotto voce, with feeling: erotization OF erasure) Meanwhile, in the back room, Nikei average down (swan's, cf pilt-) with trousers... cf odalisque w/_____. W/index. O say can you see.

"MEANWHILE IN THE IMPERIALIST WORLD OF WHICH MY PROJECT IS A PART" (enter houseboy, stage left) Armchair terrorism: talking about, not to, subjects. Subjects of the queen. (off with HER head, of course). Subjects of the study. Manhunt. Me Jane. Subjects of the discourse, ah. The search for intelligent life. The quest to turn desire into discourse. The hegemony of librarians. The briars that scratched out Rapunzel's lover's eyes. Briar Rose. Snow White. Rose Red. The desire to turn discourse into love. Emotions as contingency in social relations. Contingency as motor of history. Model T. T-cells. Once upon a Time. The

Garden Lost. The rage that is in grief. Who dies in the end. Came such a one. The flaming sword. The sword in the stone. The sword in the lake. The Ace of Swords. What is knowledge vs. what do we want to know.

Who will love me?

Artifacts. Treasures. Tropes. The Lone Ethnographer rides again. Hi ho, Bronze Age. How the west is won and won. And all alone and ever more shall be so. Othering. Point of departure for universal transcendence, said he. Simian Orientalism. Said—who? Gasp, she! *Comme* Tonto, Sancho and Babalooee, the _____s three. (Yoruba meets Disney, admission free). On Donner, on Blitzen. (etc., some more.) Krieg. Flieg. (Zeus at it again). Fiddlers three. Mouseketeers, raise yr ears. Hermes, let yr wand alone. You, too, Prospero, of which yr project is a part. Daddy, let yr mind roll on. Yo, Tarzan.

EVERYBODY'S TALKIN BOUT A NEW WAY OF WALKIN

So where are the tropes of yesteryear? *Trauer arbeit.* (again, more.) The work that is in grief. The "out there" life is formulated against. Death. Mr. D. Management courtesy Judeo/xtian science. Travel arrangements provided by Kodak. Photograph as presence as absence. *Trauer arbeit.* Vs. the panoptical gaze. Who steals my look steals no/thing. I looked over Jordan and what did I see? (perfect postmodern man. hey look me over. four-leaf clover. Irish eyes. smile of the medusa. slithering.) (artifacts treasures tropes) The veil rent. (troping toward Bethlehem) *Primate Visions.* Coming for to carry me home. Voluntary entry in flow of spirit. You will never walk alone. (you Jane)

(Who authorizes the questioning of authority? Arguably it's an excellent thing. ("this is my feeling about it")) My fair lady. My girl Friday. Nat'l secretaries week. Pretty woman. Annie, get yr gun. (Foul(colt) 45) Koko get her kitten (fine gorilla animal). (LIVE LIVE LIVE) Get yr own mirror. Bette Davis eyes.

Desinit In Piscim / A Fish Tale

Forget science. The children of frost
(*little matchgirl in transubstantiation—Jakob Boehme*)

are at home among the Japanese. A shallow land
(windowpane, counterpane)

is strange, just cause
(*Operation Clockwork Orange*).

Those snow
(coked)
(Blake's chimneysweep: O but my soul is white!),

Pacific O
(conquest, a popular thing to think about).

Flag, civilization, grass skirt harvest.
(Slash and Burn: serial killer is code
for Rape and Torture women.
The latest: rape rates up 59% this year.
But not to worry; overall number
"still RATHER SMALL")

Mine: NOblesse Oblige, DrOit de Seigneur, etc. Tariff. Wave.
(WAV)

flak Raft george Mote saint Beam male-mal-mail
(will not stray from appointed etc)
Draft blind/blond eye Ocean na(pal)m oven Omen.

Body
(water/land)

question.
(Newton's. Niemans. Sci-fides. Well-sempered)

A poet will regress the seasons
(Jews born-again of smoke);

chemistry as livelihood is an improvement
(yet Primo Levi jumps):

electricity and vinegar
(through a straw)
for dinner of an eve.

"I had lost my physicality." True progress forget soul
(its transparent habit)

"having a swallow like flight and insectivorous habits"
(Metamorphosis, Ovoid and Kafkoid)

the big gulp
(Lust belongs to the Egg);

upon examination
("PUR SI MUOVE": Galileo, sotto voce,
on his knees before the Inquisitors,
a game of dominoes) an Italian invention

we find evolution of the lazy and warm
(O tempora! O mores!)

to the level of the knee
(O altitudo!).

Information is French; they destroy the habit
of the subject
(the soul of dirt)

its tongue its calm
(mane tekel phares)

its newspaper the pedestrian who doffs
his hat. Wax candle
(mehr licht mein gott)

north garden
(give lilies)
the elements

the century is just possible, a fish climate for justice
(You, sirrah, teach a fish to swim),

scales awash. *Sublata causa, tollitur effectus:*

Justice Notice/slow burn

girls, grails, god in heaven
sad by hope>product
(will bloomSunday)
Boston a pain>trill requires
rrr practice, sample birds'
anxiety mode>a la Jane a
name like fingernails
a woman just ice
goes on>the extinct wings
the murder age ours, those
disappeared krill
willing>>killing
music, my stave, my spine
they discomfit me>need to
bed transitive>verb like
wearing the ozone hole
emperor, brand, flank, trademark
banana republican sword/sward
<man>drill> pilipino econo
con>mode comfort girl
faint dust junk>estrus
cash flow>green fatigue
shop special, how she
stood and stood>to lose to live
the history of>promise
of>good death of

tree of ash of
praise>of prayer>of plot
dispersal

parsifal, the drop of blood
no justice no no—
not us no more n>eve>r

Taking The "Riot" Personally

On tv the black men are kicking the white now. Everybody's sinuses are stuffed from burning sofas. The President suggests we all sing "Away In A Manger." *"poor baby wakes/no crying he makes"* I am putting my belongings in storage and I don't know where to go. Tuesday and Thursday are ruined, you might as well know. I want to see her to be the way I am with her and also because I like like how she is. Ok, eek it out: I love her and but I assume she does not want to hear this. On his knees like proposing the man blind with his own blood paws the air. The image, as in the I Ching: girl, three, penis shoved down her throat. *"crib for his bed/lays down his sweet head"* Only I only dreamed about pawing the air. She was watching a video about Samoan gangsters in LA. Booming and zooming/Belonging and burning. When did "gang member" become "gangster"? (Just Say No To Welfare) Now they are a movie, pinstripe, prohibition, dinosaur cars. I didn't move then. So now I move all the time. Now I live in Solana Beach, California. Seeing "Los Angeles" on the freeway signs makes me feel like I am in a tv show. Since 1974 I haven't spent a year in the same place. 18 years, half my life, be-loning. Cairo, Istanbul, Lisbon when I was 18. I almost jumped ship, land and water, borning. "Apparently Yemen is an unusual country, all the people eat a hallucinogenic root," she sd. She sd she wants to have taught there when she could have and didn't. To live in a world that could burn down and did and you live in the ashes and it could happen again, you expect it, people who don't know you could do violence to you at any moment, that is where I live all the time. Every time I turned on the tv, I cried to see the 2-way hatred anger mirror that burns my own house down. Endure, endure till you can't no more. *"till morning is nigh(t)"* When is my turn? the thyroid asks. I want mine. I want somewhere to be long.

Descartes Ruins The World

ore bodies. (dig and delve). eel skin. (slip the light fantastic). cro-magnets. (easily d(r)awn). gollum. (jewel of the blue pacific). golem. (an it hurt none). golan. (90210).

a self-hood that is essentially affiliative

ERGO

Last known address: 1041 Factory Place, LA/CA

("It's not about livin hard and eatin honey sandwiches and
livin in the projects and walkin around on roaches
all day")

It furthers one to cross the great water
(His love for us can sweep the stars away)

stair
way

crumbs on table top   cotyledon
then just the table
he sits across and says the color at the edges of my eyelids is
the color of my lips

I knew this.
I was pleased to be seen.

*

LA: milinary and police authorities.
wingtip shoes, shies, the better to dance
on yr forehead, my dear. feather in his cap.
civil rights, friendly skies, united-not-
divided. set her cap but got no head. sad.
"of course it wasn't very lady-like for her to
lick her hand" {another bodice I mean
bone in the throat of the u.s. economy}
meanwhile back at the table. tea. celadon.
ceylon. black mesa. con.ed./m.div. el rey,
his broken crown. horses, men, together
again: careful with that axe, eugene.
careful with that juror.

Pensee 253. Two extremes: to exclude
reason, to admit reason only.

The hammer is as old as nails.

*

The efforts have been made. There are worse efforts pending. The
letters explaining exactly how come back address unknown. I only
know how to have addressed you then

now. (some think the angels wd be jotting this down) now
an important message for you from the makers of time:

                    *
                         *
*

         *

                                   *

)

...asking you to do something scary for yourself (lightning lighting the way to her mama's bed: "sometimes the things that scare us most get us to a place that's safe." I do not feel safe. U.S. Justice Dept.: domestic battery most significant cause of injury to women (not about livin hard and his love can sweep again she says "I love you" again and Mel Gibson hits her again

)),turn off the tv.
COGITO

got hit with the ugly stick "if I were a girl I'd be stupid and weak as a string" guess (jeans) who "it's a wonderful thing to be talking about business and freedom"—geo bush. Corporate Living, the magazine. Maquiladora Monthly. "the beehive has been proven to be more sterile than a modern hospital. the beehive with its 100's of occupants smells fresh and clean at all times" (I read it on the gum wrapper).

depilatory

racial

cleansing

deodorant tampons

rape

camps

douche

counselors

the efforts have been made
(le coeur a ses raisons)

"take her away, she has hair around her nipples!" —*Bear*
the juicy fruiting of the trees
"choice: get exceptionally vague or be dogmatic"
consumer durables: "garbage is an item of commerce, therefore
states may not say no"
imagine having to insist no means no
bird means bird
excessive force means
how many times do you have sex you don't want
("blowin in the wind")

"Well, Mr. Raper he did it anyway and then said it just happened":
testosterone redux. quack. discontent as content, accent on the con.
Untied States. All her soul's shoelaces undone when she went out
into the day from that bed. Who will understand this? Her self
came un affiliate. (stats may not say no)

*

Pensee 292. He lives on the other side of the water.
Pascal eats Chinese.

*

1,028: the number of stars, according to Ptolemy's catalogue.

*

"On November 10, 1619, a 23 year old began to create a system of
thought, a scientific method, that would serve to shed light on all
objects of human inquiry, whether in the realms of mathematics,
philosophy, or biology."

1. There were 23 yr olds in 1619, imagine.
2. He thought he could do this.
3. Many for long thought he had done this. Imagine.

1. *pulsion*
2. *attouchement*
3. *pensee*

*

From his correspondence with Elizabeth (effectrix) concerning the union of mind and body, 6 May, 1643:

>you and yr *notions primitives* (D to E)
>*nous experimentons* (E to D)

*

>I find I have written on the frontispiece of my 1981 copy of *The Essential Descartes* which was in a box in an Ohio attic from 1982-90, an Ohio basement 1990-92, then a garage in Pacific Beach for two months, then a storage bin in La Jolla for 6 weeks, now in New Mexico, on my desk: "*meta*, after/ *odos*, road: going on a path"
>>and

"her eyebrows are like little clouds over the sea".

>This is why I do not have a Ph.D.
>(*esprit de fin/esse de siecle*—anon.)

*

Failure of imagination is generally what is meant by sin. Imagination moral faculty. x=x where guess what, Woman, "to use a math term, has no symbol, doesn't exist." Lady luck smiles like the Chesire cat at this.

*

crows in plowed field today. crumbs on table top. I said I was a marble rolling around on the table top of the world; somebody liked this, I can't remember who. cro-magnets: their beaks can't help it, just happens. ore bodies: mamacita. affective affinities. the efforts—no honey sammiches. nada. fresh and clean at all times.

That which is extended is an object occupying place.
A body possesses extension.
It just happened, he said.
The extended is extended.
Mind is entirely indivisible.
I Me Mine/LA
(and he said unto himself let me go out unto all the
world an multiply)

*

The desired ("I'm in love with Alec Scudder." "What a groteque announcement"), the clear and distinct idea: "supposing every extended object in the universe were annihilated, that would not prevent extension in itself alone existing." Scud missile. Let x=x. Final Solution (with meticulously kept records, *quel surprise*).

1. Imagine believing this.
2. Look around, see they do, they get it and prove it on you.
3. This is how they say I or me or mine (ultra affiliative or not at all?)

*

The little wing bug
on the same peeling inch of window sill all day;
outside snow, a piece of white bread.
Where are you?
How to know?

*

    esprit de geometrie   rain
    wept

SUM

that one   and   this
intermingled   there is
   light   the unnumbered   stars
 are not   swept
away

Character

—for Marian Engel, her *Bear*

i.

Gr. χαρακτηρ; from verb meaning
to make sharp, to cut into
furrows, to engrave.

      1. a sign...a mark

          3a. appearance...as token of real nature
          b. Cath. Theol. The spiritual mark impressed on
          the soul...
          by which the recipient is...marked for the worship
          of God.

ii.

Equation Mark Twain	Charles' Wain
two wain	the moondoest
to wane	going once, going twice
to bear	cart, wagon, carry
to bear	violent, it, away
to bare	bark mark
too bare	stark mark

too star	night sky
two star	scar scry
= little dippers	heaven (bear) this cup=
drink two deep	gulp heaven gulp

iii.

THE LINE FROM SCAR TWO SCAR A LIFE
DOES MAKE, BEAR, LOVE.

Forms Of Address

"Evening and morning, the first day."
—Genesis

...   *Evening and morning, the first day*

He lets there be the sense of *yeah*—
well, he lets there be that.

Heartened like a bird would be
a feeling in the hollow bones.

Yearning makes the heart deep
heart deep.

(Heard the gate latch sound, looked, someone coming, I thought
it love coming up my stairs. I do this, I have, for many years, the
lost ones returning, need blooms its recompense. But no, it wasn't,
it wasn't ago. "No mirror, no light, no home, no prayer.")

...   *Evening and morning, the second day*

"I don't like this kind
of houses; I like that kind
of houses."

(o syllable o footfall—
she don't know where to go)

... *Evening and morning, the third day*

If all we have is our choices, what kind of having do we have?
Touch but don't know, the hand, the reach, the I, opening a
meaning...

(*Reine de jadis:* the child afraid, rubbing spit into the golden hallway
wallpaper needing pencil mark to go away. Parents hate each other
for loss of Miss Romper Room career. A mirror they see through
pretending to see you, a mouth in a frame with fringe,
photogenetic language of a world of beings *utterly unaware of
spiritual need* always ready to (brother uncle, what big finger
tongue you have) eat.)

... *Evening and morning, the fourth day*

The tomb in Cairo, the night sky arcs her body, her belly full of
stars a canopy above the forever bed of grave. Old man whose face
I would not see wanting gives me the Justine tour of Alexandria.
The cabs, hansom, pedi, going. "Don't thank me; the car you are
riding in is not mine." True of the entire world, for that matter.

(What the bees know. So always some have eaten and some have
starved. Some have the blessing of pollen. Some have been eaten
(and it's Gretel 1 by a length; handsome is as handsome does). All
steer by songlines in the sun.)

...   *Evening and morning, the fifth day*

I don't know where to go.

(I know the magnetic language of loss, learned that first going I don't know how to say—QED.)

...   *Evening and morning, the sixth day*

"There is no difference between your book and mine." Could it be true? (do)

("Gold is heavier than silver; wood is lighter than iron; am I right?")
...dull sublunary sphere...

Eve

I want, I want. "Rain, when will you rain down?"—Baudelaire's swan so names himself. "And the grass grassed forth grasses:" in the beginning the end was not so far, language and the body closer and home, evening and morning, the first day words. Show your hand. Who ever you are. Touch my face, night sky, night sky.

Mourn

     "Where is that poor girl going?"
     Poor thing. At a distance, through leaves.

She Sang

words so long
they shut the door
of earth in her face

so long

as if the world
had grown a skin

she touched

lattice work of wanting
that makes up the wombs of rain

how it embraces itself
and gives itself away

~
~

s/he

("since I was little, I was waiting
a sign from the eye of earth
a heaven for the livid
freedom vegetable
new capitalist trash

the eastern-most belly of Mass Cash
seedling sun, sunset sprout
water table paramount, oh")

sang

clouds so low, Nathan Perch
came to rest in a 4-star
cumulo-nimbus nation
(her dream of fish in sky)

~

~

is

there a word in the house
to open the house's door?

as if

the world had grown a skin she touched

skin listens
[and here the wor(l)d touches back]

ii.

...thus we are—and we know not how: there is something
in us that can be without us and will be after us; though it is
strange that it hath no history what it was before us.
—Sir Thomas Browne

What requires food is not eternal.
—Aristotle, *Metaphysics*

Some say say she do and some say she dont.
—Blues tune

Black Agitator, I Want To See Your

This is about

sex.   You

could tell?

THE EPONYMOUS   ANCESTOR OF THE PHOENICIANS
AND FATHER OF EUROPA

o syllable o footfall

her home was a very cold place she is sitting alone,

mellifluous

(New, Improved) Strange Matter

Scientists! Do you, when you sit in the theater, exercise slight but persistent pressure against your neighbor's offending arm that usurps the armrest, and this with the air, so to speak, of one who has farted: that is, the air of the innocent, neither involved in nor responsible for the effects of your body's endeavor?

Unusual forms of matter may be arriving at Earth in the form of cosmic rays. I quote *Science Magazine. At* Earth. Interesting choice of prepositions. You could turn to your neighbor and whisper this, with that same air of unconsciousness, so that he might not be certain whether you are in fact addressing this remark to him. Whether he is, in fact, the intended recipient of this pronouncement. Whom you intend. She, rather.

Or, more economically: *I hope I don't have teeth like that.* (Furthermore, he may never know you quote from "Son Of Frankenstein" at him. Her, rather.)

So, ah… I was just—wondering. A lot of people spell that 'wandering', as in "I was just wandering". Maybe they mean it, maybe they are. How should I know, who read other peoples' mail, what their erring correspondents mean. This is all just to say if not demonstrate that I have sympathy, O physicists, for you. "One part of my heart is sorry for you yet," or however it goes, what Lear says in the storm to the fool on the hill (here Sergio Mendes and Brasil 66 rise like Orion above the horizon of my life there at the point I was 16 or so, there in the South where we Sir and Ma'am each other and I, a girl, was being Sir'd; in fact, what rises is their album cover, the naked woman decorated with whipped cream, her nipples covered, in these United States (for we are considering the geography of the woman's body, there are men standing on it wielding instruments with intent to claim, king, poke, name, how not, what else, but of course; a fanfare for king and country, please Columbus), with a golden sticker. Figure it: on your back, whip-cream covered, men walking around on you? Terra firma for Orion, that original walker-stalker, his sword)). Because, hey, quark theory's great, but: "no experiment using particle accelerators has ever produced unequivocal traces of quarks." Physicists, I know what it's like. As they say in reggae, who feels it, knows it. Easy in the islands, islets of Langerhans. Lagoons. Loons. Horns. Horn Island. (Hornbill) Brass. (Admiral). Butterfly, path of, please see. Cloud chamber. Chamber music. A room of cirrus melodies. Traces. Aces. Gifts. You, she said. He, by then, rather. Are a gift to me. And then I moved to California.

The printed page somewhere sometime insisted: "Planet" is from a Greek verb meaning to wander. Myself, I have lived in eleventen states in eleven years. Myself, I have always thought that Meno is like Little Nemo but with Big Meaning and Tarzan-centric claims to positivist papa-dom floating around the edges, connoting. As in: Wake up, wake up, sleepy slave-boys, and know. Myself, I've also enjoyed the fact that, not being British, I say and hear those around me also not being British say Playdoh for Plato. Playdoh, you know, kidstuff comes in yellow cans, comes in blue green yellow and red. Playdoh. When speaking of The Forms, this is good, don't you think? *He looked upon what he had made and called it good.* And wasn't it good (asked the more modest demi-urge), that salty taste, that certain smell? (O Tiamat, my salty love, where ARE you? Done in by another walker-stalker w/sword, alas...). Yes, the unexamined life is not worth, etc. But (a silence sodden with shame again) I examine mine too much.

I can't stop. Apparently. Unequivocal traces, car 54, *ou etes vous? I wonder as I wander out under the sky. Why Jesus our savior came down for to die.* (Arriving at Earth in the form of comic I mean cosmic, etc.) He used to sing that. I have carried around in my wallets (they fall apart, things do, me, too) all these years a small piece of paper I found in my mailbox one day saying <u>I love you I love you I love you in blue ink</u>. And it was. And to think I told him he couldn't; I thought I was stalked enough as it was.

We are wallets all to hold the loss. Loss and longing, I eat them for breakfast. Champion the lost cause: come back. And read in a letter with toast crumbs he comes to California soon. Arriving at Earth, etc. Love, love lost.

Otherwise, it's just one revelation after another, love. (Here Lloyd Cole sings: *Love, I don't let that stuff in my house.* Sing it, Lloyd.) Love. That's what our stamps say. That's the position the Americans normally occupy. Love thy neighbor; do not begrudge him your share of the arm rest. As in: Unless I have charity, though I speak with the tongues of angels, it's all brazen tongues. He once called me a Jezebel, I think. No Biblical knowledge involved. Bible. Belt. Babel. Tongues, speaking in. (Here "Burning Down The House" plays). Larks' in aspic. Birds in perspex. Quarks in love.

Charm school. Finished. Veneer. Vermeer. Pap smear and so back to charm school and so back through the ovum to Eve; back and back, every thought, every platelet swimming back and up and into and through (choice of prepositions, etc.). A strange charm guides them, the navigating salmon and the dancing bee, even the anxious ants' tracks scored these, the musics of the heavenly spheres (brass section discretionary), Provencal minstrelry Santiago Compostella Languedoc—after Aprille's showeres, the pilgrimage: REM, like Orpheus with his lute—slumber and song, singing the world into being, a la Dreamtime, all aboriginal, we go. We wander, no?

Or I do. That's it; you have (or I do) the theory etched into your (my) body, like that Kafka story, spelled out with my own blood. Spelled in, rather—the key word to open all locked-boxed key words. This word, the sound of it trembles my neutrinos and I hear only via its frequencies, I see only via its wave patterns and what a *via dolorosa* it is: nobody no not not ever never no no no never no one ever ever no no love because, Q.E.D. So again and again: *What a terrible storm, what dreadful lightning*, when all it was was a Potentially Life-giving Collision between particles, but all and each and always translated into evidence for the theory: *It's a shame I'm so* _____ (sing, heavenly Tanita), it's a shame I'm so mum. Heinrich von Frankenstein, maker of monsters, sir, you got nothin on me.

How to rearrange my leptons, spell something different, hear something new? All this translational space-time invarance is tough on a girl. So yes, I counsel a little girl raped, what in such a world can she say who has been silent so long? I quote: *Somebody ran off with all of my stuff.* (You damn right, Ntozake). And: I would like to take your arm. Not off, as he did (I feel sick when I think of him hitting you who you are), but in hand. Interesting choice of. Wonder out into the evening. Watch the movie of the stars. Hear the waves generate ( ) new theory. Issue an(d) invitation: please to join me in creating an unusual track in my cloud chamber. Exercise slight but persistent pressure, dear empiricist. (Here the waves generate...) On my body of theory. Of. At. To. For. With. In the body. Is the word.

O scientist, O lover, a quark is belief, not theory.

iii.

I will write upon her my new name.
—*St. John the Revelator*

A Poetics

Nib, n. 1. A bill or beak.
  2. The point of a pen.
  3. A pointed part; a point; a prong. "The little nib or fructifying principle." —*Sir Thomas Browne*

Here are shadows of geranium, my grandmother-totem. Pen and hand write into them, ivy-leaved geranium, yellow dirt from beachtown street in vein-valleys of leaves which were somebody's garbage. Valley of shadow of.

I am impatient with so much telling. I want, I don't want to, Death.

Instead, the night doctor. *Nihil ex nihilo.* Miniature conceptual disaster. Like immaculate conception. Like *deus absconditus*? Who would think such a thing? Why hiding, why not doesn't exist? An erosion, teeth yellowing, then no teeth, no belief. *Deus jaune.* Like yesterday's newspaper, like old sheets. A-bed, the jaundice doctor. How I lay in the hospital bed three days with fever 105, and he came and put his hands between my legs saying You must tell me everything you did with boys or you might die. Like this, like this? The official story's his, his nibs'.

Then he went on vacation.

It was a school-friend's father, after, making his urologist rounds, who looked in to see me and said: yellow as a pumpkin, hepatitis, girl. So christened, I went into a coma, my liver tired of its Mexican diet of tequila, orange juice, and puffy bread from the panaderia. When I got out of bed two months later, I never told, I went right back to never telling, to melting the contents of capsules in spoons held over matches, needling into my veins. *Nil admirari*, natch. *Nihil ex nihilo*, one night my lips turned blue. Tell who?

Botched doctor, your bill is past due.

Stoic: *nil admirari*. Silent: *nil nove sub sole*. "Why The Classics?": Elvis lives, Wm. Kennedy Smith "innocent". *Nuova Vita*, sure thing: bar of soap in my mouth; "white basin, basin blanc," *mange, essen, kinder, essen*. Sing it now: W*hoops, there goes* ("We got low hopes, we got no hopes..."), *whoops there goes another rubber plant tree*. Veritable plantation. (And he said to himself, go forth unto all the earth and colonize.)

Invitation.

> At the very bottom of the photograph forest, the tiny child barefoot on the forest road looks and looks, frozen in 1962 forever. The trees are too big, the child is too small, the child is alone. What will happen? Wonder is the beginning of all philosophy—Plato. Wonderful (terrible), *deinos*, is man—Sophocles. To and fro,

over the face of the earth he goes. *Deinos*
like dinosaur. There once was a child alone
in the woods when the world's light was
nearing its end and the great trees drew
night up through their roots, breathing.
The man, crouching over. Wonder at
nothing. Keep your eyes on that leaf and
un-know, forever. Never say. But dream
the little inner dream and don't know what
it means for thirty years and more—when
at last you look up from the leaf into
somebody's eyes and see. And begin to
know what it means to know what it
means. Spit it out. Say—so the seasons
return, so the dead leaf dies. And ceases to
mean.

Nature is a temple whose living pillars
sometimes let a confused word fall—
Baudelaire. In the garden was an apple
tree and at its foot sat a maiden in whose
lap the unicorn rested its head. In the
garden was the knowledge tree, in the
garden was the great ash, Yggdrasill.
Yclept Waldner, forester, tree-keeper, my
father was, and his, and I. I keep the count
of days, I tell the leaves, with these keep
hope green. In this way I make them and
they make me a spoken word: Be.

Melizalphabet

1. I always especially liked too when she spreads her paw and "wharshes inbetween the mechanisms," even better now I know the nambes of all that (being).

2. Did you call them typologisms?

3. *Ensure* its wonderfulness" or more like corroborate or ascertain or on the other hand like insure which would ensure your position as demi-urge in this (or any) poesis business, which position you can't think about too much in your line of work, yesno?

4. In the hollow of left external nare my absent-minded finger just discovered a pimple that made its appearance sometime while we were on the sandbar, I reckon, since it wasn't there, at least not to my finger's knowledge, while smearing said nare with sunscreen earlier. Here's the thing: I had no idea and why not? There I was, threshing salty waters, mirating at the wide sky, and somewhere within me, neutron said let there be pimple and there was pimple and it strikes me as weird not to have a clue, I dunno. Are they I mean we happy in there/here?

5. in, "erudite in happiness" ("with 0 learned")
("all the cl0uds turn t0 w0rds, all the w0rds
fl0at in sequence, n0 0ne kn0ws what they
mean, every0ne just ign0res them").

6. Chimeric genes are the newly invented composites ("with 0 learned"). The stuff dreams are made on. This always sounded messy as though

a) symptomatically
b) schematically
c) spermatic a la wet dreams and or dreamsicles and men in leggings.

7. **fascicles**: n. pl.: little bunches (fasces) of fatty acid sacs which are like something. see also **fascioun**: Chaucerian codpiece, the height of, in its (hay)day (see diddle, etc); riding to hounds, houndstooth, horehound: so many young vowels so easily nouned (see also **tup**)

8. say right here what you've found to be
complicatedly magical in a funniness:

(a) place to say
b) place for saying
c) place for to say *
d) plus fours (four of swords)
e) plaice
f(in)

*Emily get yr gun, my life had stood a
loaded, buffalo gals in Amherst, et al.

9. *it's awl I'm talking about* (Punch and Judy make st=ars in their respective sk/(e)y(e)s)

(a jerkin, a leathern, a cocktail shaker, The Nun's Tale)

10. formal malaria: tuxes, trochees and quinine of an afternoon; sweaty upper lip and dreamtime sonnets meet all syllogistically in you: if not hay, then bee, wouldn't you say, Smoothfield?

11. "where sips the bee, there sip I"

prithee
take me
where

                    "let me bring thee
where crabs grow and I with my long nails
will dig thee pine-nuts show thee a jay's
nest and instruct thee how to snare the
nimble marmoset..."

12. but I am the queen of memory.

La Reine de Jadis used to be...
"when thou first camest thou strokedst
me, wouldst give me water with berries
in't and teach me how to name the bigger
light and how the less that burn by day
and night: and then I loved thee..."

13. wd you be surprised to know I know
many portions of many Emily Dickinson
poems by heart?

14. Maybe I will change my name to Trail. But then I couldn't move to Albuquerque and have a dog and a pick-up and hang out at ARF (it's a question of taste) (salty lips and all)

15. "O Perfect Masters, they thrive on disasters": ED's Master Letters? ED.D: Emily Dickinson, Dominatrix. School For Scandal, natch. History is an interruption in what, may I ask. You mean in just how you go along being, how we rest in our being and then comes some guy with a who's who and a pen or a story? Kennebunkport, home of

a) Elvis and the Ancient Greeks (is this a century fibrillating?)

b) Perfect Masters Playoff

c) Purloined Native American remains

d) The Bush clam

16. I don't have a clue why should I

(courtesy Kennebunkport Bush wire service)

(see also: 'they just haven't heard yet in Darien' etc)

17. What does it look like when it happens, centuries fibrillating? Or how does it feel, if that is the question that will let me know what you are meaning. Is this something to do with Tenochtitlan time?

18. The tall ships arrive in Boston tomorrow. Schooners sailed past here on their way. I saw them from the rock where Miles Standish proclaimed the existence of the Massachussetts Bay Colony. Is this a fibrillation? The African Meeting House on Beacon Hill (SHIPS, p. 30) is remembering tall ships carried slaves. I am remembering the biggest genocide in the interruption of the world, courtesy tall ships. Ire service: the rage that is in grief. "History is not the totality transcended by eschatology, metaphysics or speech. Hisotr=== is transencence istself

19.   Stub   born   Sub   born
Wave born Aphrodite
              (a shoot from Jesse's stock
the Goddess
              Osiris
re-emerges
              the green man)

20. wood wind the gentle
(read genetic)

21. Rapunzel rappel rape is what
she ate who stood it all

Demeter swallowed it hole
which wanting to climb?
how to leave your mind alone
(cf the musical

a) plea
b) injunction
c) advice: Daddy let yr mind roll)

22. Moodem.

23. I don't know how to fax
(*she. came. from. planet. claire.*)

24. Heavens to murgatroid.

25. not really
(Ground Control to Major Tom (*at Earth*))

26. "And Being But An Ear" omigod again
and still

to vibrate in the wind of all being, to be
the breath of what is being said, and being
said, is created—in the beginning was *o
logos* and *o logos* was/with god who said let
there be light and there was light: shining
out of his mouth through the snakes in the
g and the cave of the h; and thus to be a
word that is becoming, each movement of
your mind of your will of your body of your
imagination trembling the membrane of
Being's Ear, tapping out the code on the
web of all being, breathing the breath of
the Creation, the being-shaped air
brooding over the face of the waters, the
inner ear the sacred sea; spelling, Sweet
Bee, with the days of your life the sounds
of your secret name, writing with your life
in the book of days the sounds that means
you, (passing from reaching for the faucet
in the sink of our being through the
tympanum into being known, into the
feeling of meaning)—oh it's spelling, it's
singing the names that make/s us be

26. Amen, love—
                    me

Notes

ETYM(BI)OLOGY: Athena Trasha declined and conjugated (in several senses) from Ronald Firbank, writer, d. 1926 (Dalkey Archive Press). See the unwittingly _____ bio @ theknittingcircle: lit; "The sunstroke he suffered as a child left him delicate. He also spent much of his time alone."

Lawrence Durrell of *The Alexandria Quartet*, in "Forms of Address" too.

Of this poem and the book as a whole, Helene Cixous': "Hold still, we are going to do your portrait so you can begin looking like it right away." (*Laugh of the Medusa*)

_____

ANGR: "Representation of the world, like the world itself, is the work of men; they describe it from their own point of view which they confuse with absolute truth." Simone de Beauvoir (*The Second Sex*)

_____

STILL LIFE II: For a class-and-gender-sensitive analysis of how fact is constructed, inflected, and policed, see Donna Haraway, her *Primate Visions*.

Judy Nylon/man what couldn't afford to orgy: John Cale singer and song.

"Feminism has a theory of power: Sexuality is gendered as gender is sexualized. Male and female are created through the erotization of dominance and submission. ...there is no ungendered reality or ungendered perspective." —Catharine A. MacKinnon, *Toward the Feminist Theory of the State*

————

DESCINIT IN PISCIM : Who gets to witness it, who gets to tell it, and in what words? Government control of media during Gulf War: as usual the rape of women "civilians" not worth mentioning, even as "collateral damage."

Galileo: *pur si muove*: it does too move

mehr licht: supposedly Goethe's last words/ more light

sublata causa...: remove the cause, the effect is washed away

JUSTICE NOTICE: "sex tourism," the outrageous phenomenon and the outrageous term, co-depenent products of global capitalism ("GE brings another good thing to mehr licht")

"for which/like anmesiacs in a ward on fire, we must/find words/or burn —Olga Broumas, "Artemis"

DESCARTES RUINS THE WORLD: Descartes' positivist project affirms male interest (subjectivity) as objective reality/truth (and control over nature/women as political foundation of state, promulgated by 'culture') Media promotion of romantic hetero love its method; method never neutral; battering seen as evidence of this love/reality: damage ontology: he hits me therefore I am.

CHARACTER: Charles' Wain is another name for the constellation the Little Dipper/Ursus Minor/Little Bear

Bear: Marian Engel's novel.

BLACK AGITATOR: 'o syllable o footfall' from a Susan Howe poem.

(NEW, IMPROVED) STRANGE MATTER: "It is theory which decides what we can observe" —Einstein

_____

A POETICS: "...male dominance is perhaps the most pervasive and tenacious system of power in history... Its point of view is the standard of point of viewlessness, its particularity the meaning of universality. Its force is exercised as consent..." —MacKinnon

_____

MELIZALPHABET: features language from artist Melissa Smedley

and from: Wallace Stevens: "erudite in happiness with nothing learned" —"Of Bright And Bluebirds And The Gala Sun"

Brian Eno: "all the words float in sequence..." from *Another Green World* "o perfect masters..." from *Here Come The Warm Jets*

B-52's: "she came from planet claire"

Shakespeare: from *The Tempest*, Caliban, esp; "let me bring thee... when thou first camest..."

Liz Waldner is the author of *Self and Simulacra, Homing Devices, A Point Is That Which Has No Part*, winner of the Iowa Poetry Prize and the Academy of American Poets Laughlin Prize for 2000. Her chapbooks include *Call, Read Only Memory, With the Tongues of Angels*, and *Memo (La)mento*. Published in journals such as *APR, Ploughshares, VOLT, The Colorado Review* and *The Lesbian Review of Books*, her work has received The Poetry Society of America's Robert M. Winner award; grants from the Massachusetts Cultural Council, the Lannan Foundation/Centrum and The Barbara Deming Money for Women Fund; and fellowships from the Djerassi Foundation, Hedgebrook, Vermont Studio Center, and MacDowell, among others. She lives in Seattle.